Collins

CHELP
and
CHUNTER

William Collins' dream of knowledge
for all began with the publication of
his first book in 1819. A self-educated
mill worker, he not only enriched
millions of lives, but also founded a
flourishing publishing house. Today,
staying true to this spirit, Collins
books are packed with inspiration,
innovation, and practical expertise.
They place you at the centre of a
world of possibility and give you
exactly what you need to explore it.

Language is the key to this
exploration, and at the heart of
Collins Dictionaries is language as
it is really used. New words, phrases,
and meanings spring up every day,
and all of them are captured and
analysed by the Collins Word Web.
Constantly updated, and with over
2.5 billion entries, this living language
resource is unique to our dictionaries.

Words are tools for life. And a Collins
Dictionary makes them work for you.

Collins. Do more.

CHELP
and
CHUNTER

How to Talk Tyke

Collins

HarperCollins Publishers
Westerhill Road
Bishopbriggs
Glasgow G64 2QT

www.collins.co.uk

First Edition 2007

ISBN 978-0-00-724781-3

A catalogue record for this book is
available from the British Library.

Typeset in Martin Majoor's FF Nexus
by Thomas Callan

Printed and bound in Italy by
Lego S.p.A.

Editor: Cormac McKeown

ACKNOWLEDGEMENTS
We would like to thank those authors
and publishers who kindly gave
permission for copyright material
to be used in the Collins Word Web.
We would also like to thank Times
Newspapers Ltd for providing
valuable data. All rights reserved.

Contents

ACKNOWLEDGEMENTS

I'd like to thank the generous readers of the Yorkshire Post and the Barnsley Chronicle, and the listeners to the Mark Radcliffe show on Radio 2 who sent in their amazing words that helped to fill this dictionary; without them, this book would have been much thinner and my vocabulary would have been a lot smaller than it is now!

In that connection, special mentions must go to Bill Rhodes, David Jones, Terry Marshall, Keith Jowett, Vicky Turrell and Margaret and Graham Royles.

The Yorkshire Christmas poem first appeared on BBC Radio 4.

I'd like to dedicate this book to everybody who tries to keep local language alive and thriving, wherever that may be. Even Lancashire.

Chelp and Chunter is designed with easy browsing in mind. Most of it is self-explanatory – you don't have to read the following to enjoy the book but here is some information to help you get the most out of it.

• Headwords

All main entries are printed in green boldface type and are listed in strict alphabetical order:

attercop

aumery

• Labels

The standard parts of speech are presented in labels preceding the sense or senses relating to that part of speech.

aumery *noun* cupboard or pantry

If a particular sense of a word is restricted as to appropriatenes, connotation, subject field, region of Yorksire, etc, an italic label is given:

attercop *noun spoken in North Yorkshire, old-fashioned*

• *Etymologies*

Any etymologies are contained within square brackets, and after the definition.

[from Old English *attorcoppa* from *ator* poison + *copp* head]

• *Examples of use*

Every entry is supported by a citation from our diverse range of sources, illustrating both its currency and how it is used in today's English.

> Tha' won't go in cos' of an attercop? Tha's an attercop thissen

CHELP AND CHUNTER

I was in the Mad Geoff the barber's in
Darfield near Barnsley the other day,
getting my mop cropped. The shop
was full, and there was a low murmur
of voices. No words, you understand:
just a low murmur of voices. I'd
mentioned to Geoff that I was
compiling a new Yorkshire Dictionary
and he'd said, as he often does, 'Best of
British!'. Someone put his head round
the door and said 'Ar?' and Geoff
gestured to the full chairs and said
'No!' and the man at the door said

'Reyt' and withdrew his flat-capped head into the cold air of Garden Street.

And there, in a nutshell, is the difficulty of creating a dictionary like this.
If I could translate that little Barber Shop Exchange into standard English, it would go like this:
'Excuse me, barber, I wonder if you could fit me in before half past three ?'
'No sir, as you can see, I've got a shop full of hirsute customers!'
'Right then, my good man, I'll call back later on this afternoon!'

But that conversation was reduced to :
'Ar'
'No'
'Reyt'.

The fact is that in Yorkshire we don't talk a lot, and when we say something it's often to the point and blunt at the same time, if that's not an oxymoron. After all, the Yorkshire prayer is 'Hear all, see all, say nowt; and if tha does owt for nowt, do it for thissen'. Sound advice, if you ask me.

The other difficulty for the dictionary maker is that as well as being dour we're diffuse. At the end of that minimalist exchange in Mad Geoff's, a bloke that not many of us had seen before turned to his mate and said 'No? Did he mean Nay?' and his mate nodded. 'He's from West Yorkshire,' he explained to us South Yorkshire types, and we nodded too. Yorkshire is a huge county: one that can incorporate *no* and *nay,* and *breadcake* and *teacake* and *ginnel* and *jennel* and *tenfoot* and *silin'* and *stair rods.* And if you want to know more, open the pages and come in

and play. Or come in and laik. And
take no gorm o' me: I'm only a bit of a
doll's eead when it comes to
linguistics. Ar. No. Reyt?

aboon *preposition* above

> I kept my potty in a little cupboard aboon t'stairs

agin *preposition* against

> Like bangin' your eead agin a wall

alicker *noun* vinegar

> Does tha want alicker on them chips?

'appen *adverb* maybe, possibly

> 'Appen I'll see 'im down at that milk bar in Hotton (a line from an early episode of *Emmerdale* when it was still called *Emmerdale Farm*)

attercop *noun spoken in North Yorkshire, old-fashioned* **1** a spider **2** a peevish person; a moaner [from Old English *attorcoppa* from *ator* poison + *copp* head]

> Tha' won't go in cos' of an attercop? Tha's an attercop thissen!

*This one's all but died out – I keep
trying it on audiences and nobody's
heard of it, but a lady from Keighley
wrote to me and says she uses it*

aumery *noun* cupboard or pantry

Get some pickle out of t'aumery

backendish *adjective* autumnal

It feels a bit backendish: you'll want a top coat on

badly *adjective* ill, poorly

Mi father's badly

What wi'?

He's all reyt on hissen; he just feels badly

baht *preposition* without

Ilkley moor baht 'at – madness!

*A Baronet without any teeth would be
a Bart baht bite*

IN SEARCH OF THE ATTERCOP

The attercop moves his eight long limbs
And walks through history
  carrying his name;
The attercop spins his ancient web
From muffler's end to flat cap's neb
And attercop and spider are the same
But attercop's quite obsolete,
And that's an eight-legged shame!

ATTERCOP SKIPPING RHYME

Attercop attercop
Skip faster
Don't stop
Attercop attercop
Saw your web
In the witch's shop
Attercop attercop
Go away
You scare me more than a spider
Any day!

bairn *noun* a child, especially a toddler

> Get bairns in t'car and let's go

band *noun* string

> tee thi cap on wi this bit o band

> *My wife uses this all the time and*
> *denies it is Yorkshire Dialect: surely*
> *that's one of the definitions of dialect.*

bap *noun* bread bun. *Also* **teacake, breadcake, batch**

> does tha want dripping on that bap?

barm *noun* yeast. *Also called* **yesst**

> My mother-in-law bakes wonderful bread
> because she uses the best barm – oh yesst!

> *I reckon Barm and Gorm are not*
> *worlds apart; they're like two blokes on*
> *pushbikes racing each other down the*

*street. Just before they bump into a
wall.*

barmpot *noun* a person who is considered to be
of low intelligence

> *The question is, at what stage does a
> barmpot become a doll's eead? At what
> stage is a barmpot gormless, and at
> what stage does a barmpot's
> gormlessness slip over into full-blown
> sacklessness?*

barn *verb spoken in Dewsbury* to go

> Barn to't'chip oil?

barrow *noun* rightful concern or interest;
business

> None o' yer barrow, is it?

> *So much depends upon a red barrow,*

*as William Carlos Williams almost
said. Not many people know he was
from Heckmondwike. He kept white
chickens.*

bartled *adjective* smothered in something nasty

My snap's proper bartled today. Ah'll 'ave to 'ave a
word wi' the wife

beck *noun* a stream or brook

He tummelled in't beck

*I used to know a bus conductress called
Mrs Beck; she was really stern and if
you didn't have the right change she
would give you a clip with her Set Rite
as she walked past.*

belder *verb* to shout (something) unrestrainedly,
as if in anger or pain; to bellow

he beldered like a stuck pig!

bellusses *plural noun* bellows

> Uncle Charlie's bellusses have gone; he's
> wheezing like a budgie!

belm *noun* money

> Mi pocket's jinglin' wi' belm!

bent *noun* heath or moorland

> *I spent time on't scent o treasure on't bent,* as the
> old song goes.

biggerstang *noun* a builder's scaffolding pole

> He's as lanky as a biggerstang!

> *Surely the best word in the language?*

blaeberry *noun* a bilberry

> tha meks a reyt blaeberry pie: will tha marry mi?

blake *adjective* (of skin complexion) sallow

> He's as blake as a banana in a dim leet.

bleck *noun* thick, fatty, and dirty oil as found on axles, etc

> Mi onion soup allus turns art like bleck!

> *A triumph of onomatopoeia – you can just imagine saying it while trying to fling the stuff from your hands*

blut *noun* an elderly lady

> I nearly got knocked over by that blut on her Honda.

> *If I was an elderly lady I'd object to being called a blut.*

bocken *verb* to retch or vomit

> That lard buttie made me bocken!

> *A fine word for a horrible thing*

bockle *noun* *spoken in esp Barnsley* bottle

What my mother used to call 'lazy English', although not in my book. And this is my book!

boggart *noun* a ghost

Watch out for't boggarts in't snug o't Red Lion.

boose *noun* a partition in a cowshed

Come out from behind that boose, Norman; we know you're in theer! An' stop mooin!

Presumably because it breaks up the moos?

brass *noun* money

He'll do owt for brass!

There used to be a conductor on the Sheffield-Barnsley line who had written GIZ YER BRASS AN SHURRUP *on his money-satchel.*

brat *noun* an apron

> I allus wear a brat when I'm picking dog muck out on me booits

> *At least one Welsh person has told me that brat is also Welsh. Bbut surely then it would be Bbrat?*

braunch *verb* *spoken in South Yorkshire* to boast

> gee'or braunching will tha?

bray *verb* to hit or beat

> I'll bray thi!

brew *noun* a hill

> I'll need a cuppa when I get to the top of this brew!

> *Confuses Lancashire types when they say 'Fancy a brew?' and you reply 'Aye,*

I'll get mi booits.'

bribe *noun* an off-cut of cloth

Just wave thi bribe from't winder when tha wants me to come courting!

Brings a whole new meaning to the phrase 'the police inspector accepted a bribe'; he only wanted it to clean his Ray Bans!

brig *noun* a bridge

He's comin ower't brig.

People in Barnsley still say 'darn't Brig' when they're referring to the local village of Worsbrough Bridge.

broddle *verb* to poke around in (something)

Will tha stop broddlin' thi ear wi' that bettin' shop biro!

bull week *noun* the working week before a holiday

> I've been towin' mi lops out all bull week

> *This goes back to the days when people were paid weekly in a brown envelope. You worked particularly hard on a bull week to ensure a hefty wad for the hols.*

bunch *verb spoken in Harrogate* to kick

> Stop bunching t'ball agin't wall.

cack-handed *adjective* **1** left-handed **2** clumsy

> *As a cack-handed 'un I can vouch for the fact that if you're cack-handed you're also cack-handed.*

cat ice *noun* frozen pools of water

> Don't chuck pussy on the cat ice!

> *A word with a strange ethereal beauty*

to it. If Shakespeare didn't use it, he
should have done.

champion *adjective* excellent; first rate. *Also*
grand

> That Grand Theatre's champion

cheb *verb* **1** to throw | *noun* **2** a friend

> cheb us ower mi cap, cheb

chelp *verb* to answer back

> … and no chelpin' neither!

chuddy *noun* chewing gum

> Got some chuddy there, cheb? Meetin' lass in
> five minutes.

> *First coined in 1923 when a Mr Green*
> *from Otley tried to say 'chewing gum'*
> *with his mouth full of chewing gum.*
> *Probably.*

A YORKSHIREMAN'S LOVE POEM, ER, THA KNOWS: TO BE SPOKEN AT A WEDDING BY THE PROUD FATHER

We don't say much, us Yorkshire chaps;
We mutter and we mumble from
    under our caps
And our words are few and far between
'Cos we mean what we say and
    we say what we mean

And we save our breath for cooling our tea,
So when we finally talk, believe you me
Every word rings and sings with truth
Sharper than Uncle Frank's one tooth.

So when a Yorkshireman uses
   a word like Love
You can bet your last ferret he's got
   summat to prove
And today is a day when love's in the air
And like the best Yorkshire Puddins it's
   round not square:

Round as the ring that brings you together
Round as the circle you make
   with your hands
Round as the turning of the world, whatever
's to come in the future will be just reyt grand.

We don't say much, us Yorkshire types
Cos when we talk it's mainly guttural tripe
So here's to this couple and
  may my eloquence
Make a kind of heartfelt Yorkshire sense!

So here's to happiness, here's to love
Now give her a kiss before I give yer a shove!

chunter *verb* to mutter or mumble

> Listen to 'im, chunterin' away to hissen

claart-eead *noun* an unintelligent person

> It goes t'other way round, claart-eead!

cleg *noun* a horse fly

> *Wish I'd known that when Miss Cleg*
> *was teaching me French*

clough *noun* a ravine

> Did tha' see them chuffin' Cloughs in t'clough?

clowse *noun* a canal lock

> I'll meet thi by't clowse at ten past six

> *This word sounds like the movement of*
> *a canal lock, particularly if you say it*
> *whilst blowing into a glass of water...*

cludger *noun* toilet

Excuse me, can I use your cludger?

Yes, but only in Knaresbrough

cock loft *noun* an attic

> *One of those words that I thought was*
> *standard English until I talked to the*
> *publishers of this book. Maybe that's*
> *how dialect survives: because it doesn't*
> *realise it's dialect. There's a PhD in*
> *there somewhere. Discuss.*

codder *noun* *spoken in South Yorkshire* a team-
leader at a steelworks

Don't cod the codder!

> *A codder is above a puffler, but only*
> *just.*

cog *noun* *spoken in Morley, West Yorkshire* a

segment of orange

> Cob us over a cog

This is a Morley word, which means that if you used it in Lofthouse people would look at you Gone Out.

coil oil *noun* a place where coal is kept; a coal hole

> Tha's proper bartled in soot. 'As tha been laikin' in coil oil?

collop *noun* a thick slice (of food)

cop *verb* to catch hold of (something)

> Cop 'owd o' that

Often heard at the edge of the village cricket field just before a cry of EEEEEEEEEE!

corsey *noun* a walkway; pavement

The infamous Halifax lingerie thief was caught this afternoon when he dropped a corset on't corsey

Actually it was a basque but that doesn't sound so good

crake *noun* a crow | *verb* to crow

I couldn't sleep last neet because of all that crakin' in't trees!

creel *noun* a wooden frame suspended from the ceiling, used for drying clothes

Mind the creel! You don't want to get slapped wi' a singlet!

croggy *adverb* (riding) on the crossbar of a bike

I was croggy on mi grod...

Taken from an old traditional Doncaster song. Sadly it's all that remains. Even the tune is lost.

BLIND DATE

Meet you in the ginnel
Or the gennel
Or the tenfoot
I'll be there in a skerrik
With a rooas
In my dawky hand
'cos you're the best looking lass
in the whole of England!

Glossary

Ginnel: passage between terraced houses.
Gennel: passage between terraced houses.
Tenfoot: Passage between terraced houses.
Skerrik: very small amount of time.
Rooas: a rose.
Dawky Hand: left hand.

crozzled *adjective* (of food) slightly burnt

> This pork's nicely crozzled

cubalow *noun* *spoken in East Yorshire* an airing cupboard [from an attempt to write down the word cubbyhole, I would guess]

> 'Is home brew exploded all over t'cubalow

cumfort *noun* a tourist who is not staying long

> Reyt fed up wi these cumforts I am

> *Because, in the local parlance, they've only 'cumfor't day'*

datal *adjective* slow-witted

> *Perhaps from 'dataller', a man paid by the day to do service work in a coal mine.*

dawly *adjective* *spoken in North Yorkshire* sad or

depressed

> *One could be mardy as well as dawly,*
> *but it would be best to avoid someone*
> *who was dawly, mardy, and maungey.*
> *They were also the first three of Snow*
> *White's Yorkshire Seven Dwarfs, tha*
> *knows.*

dee dar *noun* *spoken in Barnsley, derogatory* a person from Sheffield. *See* **Dingle** [in imitation of the way that many Sheffielders pronounce the 'th' elements of dialect words such as 'thee' and 'thou']

> Can you hear the dee dars sing? No! No!
> (Barnsley football chant)

deg *verb* to sprinkle (something)

dift *verb* to extinguish (an unfinished cigarette)

for use later

> Quick, dift thi woodbine before it sets fire to't hymn book!

> *Placing behind the ear is optional. All cigarettes should be fully difted to avoid flat cap conflagration*

dimp *noun* a cigarette butt

> Look at him collecting Dimps!

> *The Dimp Difters were a Hull Punk Band.*

Dingle *noun spoken in chiefly Sheffield, derogatory* a person from Barnsley. *See* **dee dar**

> Sit down Dingle! Sit down Dingle!

> *This last is a popular football chant directed at the Barnsley manager when he is seen standing up to complain*

28

about something. The word is an
allusion to the uncouth family of that
name in the TV soap opera Emmerdale.

dixie *noun* a lookout

When I worked on a building site a
bloke was having a crafty fag and I
was put on lookout. 'If you see the
gaffer, sing dixie' said Crackerjack (not
his real name). The gaffer approached
and I began to carol 'I wish I was in
Dixie, hoorah, hoorah… ', in the
manner of Al Jolson.

dollop *noun* a lump (esp of some sort of soft
food)

would you like a dollop wi' that collop

doll's eead *noun* *spoken in Rotherham* a foolish

person

> He lost his car keys down grate; he's a reyt doll's eead

> *A nicely graphic representation of empty-headedness: a doll's head with maybe a little screw rattling around inside it. There's a whole cultural landscape here taking in doll's eeads and clartheads and gormlessness and sacklessness.*

dolly-posh *adjective* **1** left-handed | *noun* **2** a left-handed person

> My wife and I are both dolly-posh. And the vicar who married us was a dolly-posh an' all!

dowly *adjective* dismal and dull

dree *adjective* lonely, weary

Just think, if Wordsworth had come
from Shelf he could have written 'I
wandered dree as a cloud...'

dub *noun spoken in Yeadon* a puddle

> *Dun't fall in't dub!*

dummelhead *noun* a stupid or slow-witted
person

> *But not quite as stupid or slow-witted*
> *as a doll's eead*

Easter-ledges *noun* a pudding made from the
young leaves of the bistort plant

> *And also said to taste 'worse than a*
> *welcome mat' to quote a TV Chef.*

'ee by gum! *interjection* Good lord!

> *Part of Yorkshire cliché, but still spoken.*

Life imitating art, or summat. Also the method used by Yorkshire pensioners to ingest their mind-expanding drugs. Ho Ho.

ennog *noun* a back alley. *Also* **snicket, tenfoot** *or* **ginnel**

If this isn't Psychogeography then I'll stand for the Drop of York, as my wife says.

ettle *verb* to attempt

I'll ettle to fettle't metal on that kettle!

fair fahl *noun spoken in Driffield* an ugly facial expression

He had a reyt fair fahl on him when Driffield lost 10–0.

fast *adjective* stuck

I'm fast in this three-wheeler!

I'll have thi a race then

No, doll's eead; I'm fast in this free wheeler. Has tha some coconut oil and a crowbar?

fent *noun* an off-cut of cloth

A fent is smaller than a bribe.

fetch *verb* to give (eg a blow)

He fetched me a reyt scutch when I called him a dee dar

fettle *verb* to mend or tidy

Fettle me this plugoil!

finnd (rhymes with 'sinned') *verb* to find. *See* **blinnd**

I finnd I go blinnd when ah look into a leet!

flig *verb* to fly

I'm fliggin to my villa in Tuscany

Old Yorkshire Skipping rhyme:
fliggin owwer't brig
fliggin owwer't brig
fliggin owwer't brig
(repeat until exhausted or until
skipping rope snaps. Or Jocks.)

flooer *noun* a floor

Will thi gerrus some new flooer clarts at t'shop?

I like this word because it feels typically
Yorkshire; take a short word and
pronounce it differently just for the hell
of it.

flummoxed *adjective* confused

That Theory of Relativity flummoxes me...

One of the greatest words in any
language, I think

CHRISTMAS YORKSHIRE PUDDING

Ingredients:
1. Milk
2. Eggs
3. Flour
4. Santa Hat
5. Santa Beard
6. Holly, sprig of

Method:

1. Place Santa hat on head.
2. Place Santa beard on chops.
3. Say Ho.
4. Say Ho.
5. Say Ho.
6. Mix flour, eggs, and milk.
7. Mix Ho, ho and ho.
8. Put mixture in hot oven in roasting tins full of fat as hot as Rudolph's nose.
9. Wait. Hum 'Have yourself a Merry Little Christmas' seventeen times and then the puddings will be done.
10. Take puddings out of oven.
    They should be deep.
    They should be crisp.
    They should be even.

They are hard as Iron.
They are like a stone.

11. Stick the holly in a pudding.
12. Walk into the room wearing the Santa Hat and the Santa Beard, spraying weak Ho Ho Ho's into the icy silence.
13. Stare at the weeping wife, the sibbing children.
14. Apologise yet again for forgetting to buy the turkey.
15. Say Ho
16. Say Ho.
17. You know the rest....

fond *adjective* foolish

> Yer fond 'aporth!

> *I think this goes back to Elizabethan times and is a hangover from that era. Which is a heck of a hangover.*

fother gang *noun* a compartment for storing hay above a cattle stall

> I've just stored mi hay in that theer fothergang.

frame *verb spoken in South Yorkshire* (esp in the phrase frame oneself) to do one's share of work or work harder; to get oneself organized

> Come on lad, frame thissen wi' that! Tha meks no friends down here laiking about like a bairn

> *I once heard a granddad in a park say to a toddler who couldn't get onto a roundabout: 'come on, frame thissen, lad!'*

frosk *noun* a frog

> There's a frosk in my wellies!

> *frosk seems to include the sound of the*
> *frog splashing in the water, rather like*
> *Basho's famous frog haiku.*

froz *adjective* frozen

> Am froz!

> *I'm sure this came about because*
> *somebody's lips froze halfway through*
> *saying Frozen...*

fuddle *noun* spoken in South Yorkshire an
informal meal; a buffet

> There'll be a fuddle after't service

> *I've also heard a pouffe called a buffet*
> *(with the emphasis on the hard T) so*
> *you could have a fuddle and buffet in*

the middle of the buffet

gallock *adjective* left-handed

garth *noun* **1** a child's hoop, often the rim of a bicycle wheel **2** a back yard or small garden

> Where's Garth?
>
> In't garth wi' 'is garth

gawky *adjective* left-handed

> He's that gawky handed he can't right reyt!

As a left hander myself, I'm interested that there are very few words for right-handed people, even in Yorkshire!

gegs *plural noun* glasses or sunglasses [Possibly from 'goggles']

> Tha looks a reyt pip in those gegs

gennel *noun* a narrow passage way between

terraced houses

running through the ginnels wi' a telly under mi arm

See also snicket and tenfoot, although a ginnel isn't strictly a snicket and a snicket isn't quite a tenfoot. It's a philosophical/psychogeographical conundrum.

gert *noun spoken in South Yorkshire* a wife or partner

Love to join you, lads, but our gert's got the monk on about summat

I once read an article about a Sheffield dustman in The Guardian. *The journalist wrote 'Mr Barnes and his wife Gertrude' but that's not what the dustman meant when he said 'Me and*

our gert'

gie'ower *verb* to cease

Gie'ower wi' that racket

From 'give over'

gill (pronounced 'Jill') *noun* half a pint

Go on then – ah'll just have a gill.

Not many remember the old Yorkshire music hall turn 'The Gill Triplets', Jill, Gil and Gill. They liked a gill all right...

gilt *noun* a young sow

that cloud up there looks like a gilt!

ginnel *noun* an alleyway. *Also* **jennel** *or* **tenfoot** *or* **ennog** *or* **snicket**

gip *verb* to retch

them slug soufflés make me want to gip!

A remarkably powerful, almost magical
word; just writing it down and saying
it in my head makes me want to be sick
in a bowl or a bucket.

giz *verb* give that to me [A minimalising of *give it*.
Which would have become *giz it*. Which would
have become *giz*]

aw giz it! Gu on, giz it!

glimmer *noun* a young female sheep

An alternate title for this book could
have been Gilt and Glimmer,
although that does sound like a firm of
solicitors from Upperthong.

gloppened *adjective* amazed; astounded

Ah were reyt gloppened when I found a moth in

mi Yorkshire puddins!

A word that seems to mirror the
widening of eyes in astonishment.

gobblety gook *noun spoken in North Yorkshire*
leaves of field sorrel that, when chewed stimulate
the salivary glands to produce copious amounts
of drool

Tha's got gobblety gook

Interesting how something so specific
has come to mean garbled language.

goff *verb* to reek; smell horrible

By gum, tha' goffs like a groop, lad. Has tha been
rollin' in cowfield again?

Not to be confused with to Gough, to
smell like a bowler after bowling
twenty overs in hot climes.

ELOQUENT YORKSHIRE LOVE POEM

Ah love thi moor than mi jock
When tha wears that frock
Ah love thi moor than mi snap
When tha wears that cap
Wi't neb
That dives mi daft.
Ah love thi moor than mi scran
Ah'm a lucky lucky man
Ah love thi moor than mi fuddle
That makes mi feel ot round the middle
Wi thi grin
And thi chin

gone out *adverb* blankly; incredulously

> He looked at me gone out when I told him

goster *verb spoken in South Yorkshire, esp Sheffield*
to laugh

> I had a reyt goster when I heard United beat
> Rotherham

> *Sounds like laughing if you say it*
> *quickly and breathlessly dozens of*
> *times.*

grand *adjective* excellent; first rate. *See also*
champion

> eee, that parkin's grand!

gripe a garden rake

> our Ronnie were as thin as a gripe!

> *I wonder if they call it this because it*
> *grips leaves?*

grod *noun* *spoken in esp Doncaster* a bicycle

> Gettin' a new grod for Christmas

groop *noun* the drain in a cowshed

> Stephen, your bedroom's like a groop!

> *Very unpleasant indeed. Echoes the*
> *sound of cattle defecating*

guff *noun* an emission of intestinal gas from the anus; a fart

> Who's guffed in this mini?

> *Only a certain kind of fart of course.*
> *The kind you might do in chapel*
> *during the singing of a loud hymn,*
> *forgetting that verse 35 is to be omitted.*

hagg *noun* a wooded area

> let's go and run through the hagg shouting
> wooooooooooo!

GENESIS IN YORKSHIRE MINIMALISM

Nowt.
Summat.
Leets on.

Watter.
Beeasts.
Sheps. Spuggies.
Bloke.
Lass.

Tha's got nowt on!
And tha's got nowt on!

Geraaaaaaaaaat!

hod *verb* to hold [A typical Yorkshire shortening, from 'hold']

> Hod on a minute driver, me mate's runnin' for t'bus

jiggered *adjective* extremely tired

> I'm jiggered after that run through the hagg!

> *What people who go to chapel say when they mean they're buggered.*

jock *noun* *spoken in* West Yorkshire sandwiches taken to work. *Also called* **snap** *or* **bait**

> pass us me jock, Jack

jonnock *adjective* *spoken in* Doncaster genuine

> No, it's jonnock all reyt: I saw 'im buy it missen

> *A Doncaster taxi driver told me about this one, so it must be jonnock! I've no idea where this word comes from and*

the taxi driver hasn't either. But I still
gave him a generous tip.

kall oil *noun spoken in Huddersfield* a room where people gather to gossip

He's kallin' itn't kall oil

My local barber Mad Geoff as
mentioned in the introduction runs a
good kall oil; people pop in just for a
natter with, or without a trim. Kallin is
a local West and South Yorkshire word
for gossiping and a kall oil is a
variation on chip oil and coil oil.

keck *noun* a plant with a hollow stem, especially cow parsley

What has tha put a keck in my kecks pocket for?

Interesting that kecks can also mean

*'trousers' which are hollow-stemmed
too, I suppose. In fact they've got to be.*

kegs *plural noun* underwear

A full kecks and kegs outfit

(From an advert in a Hull clothiers shop, 1927)

kevel *verb spoken in West Yorkshire* to sit, lie, walk,
or stand in a relaxed manner; to lounge

Don't kevel in church my lass. Sit up straight!

*Because it sounds a bit like Bevel, it
suggests falling over sideways.*

khali *noun* sherbert

thi dandruff looks like khali!

*The stickier the better. To be khalied can
also mean to be drunk; the stickier the
better.*

HARSH WARNING IN THE FORM
   OF A LIMERICK

A southern incomer to Tong
Got his Yorkshire speyk mixed
   up and wrong
He asked for a frosk
To fill up his flask
Then me said 'My, this tea's rather strong!'

kidder *noun* a friend; mate; pal

> Nar then, kidder.

kink up *verb* to laugh uncontrollably

> That comic down club made us kink up reyt!

> *A great phrase that mirrors the kinking up of the eyes and face when laughing.*

kytel *noun* a heavy-duty coat made from coarse cloth

> Put your Kytel on, it's froz out theer!

> *Not to be confused with a 1980s popular music record label. Unless you're a doll's eead.*

laik *verb spoken in South Yorkshire* **1** (of children) to play **2** to avoid work; to skive

> Frame thissen, lad! Where does tha live? Laik district?

Another word that enlivens and enhances the language, as all words should.

latt *noun* a thin strip of wood

That new boyfriend of our Daphne is as thin as a latt!

This can be spelled either with one or two t's. Or in the case of a very very thin strip of wood, four t's: lattt. Which can also mean a thin, unappealing coffee in certain parts of the Vale of York.

leet *noun* a light | *verb* to light (something)

Leet leet, will tha?

My father in law would use the word Leet for daft, presumably from light headed.

leet geen *noun spoken in West Yorkshire* a person of low intelligence

> leet geen as a posser yed

> *I'm searching for the lost Yorkshire Play about the Doll's Eead meeting the Leet Geen*

lem *noun* **to have a lem on** to be angry. *Also* **monk**

> He's got the lem on since Barnsley lost 3–0.

lenerky *adjective spoken in Grange Moor* soft or floppy

> Your uncle Stan's gone a bit lenerky

lief *adverb* **as lief** as gladly

> I'd as lief stick pins my eyes as watch Rovers

A word that you imagine has died out but go to a pub deep in South or West Yorkshire and sit for a month and I guarantee you'll hear it.

lig *verb* to lie

> Stop liggin' abaht and get summat done

This word is still very widespread in Yorkshire and is beloved of settee makers everywhere.

linjee *adjective spoken in Beverley* (of a person) athletic

> By, that postman's Linjee: must be all them heavy parcels he carries abart!

loosie *noun* a cigarette sold singly

> Aw, giz a loosie! Come on, giz one! Come on, giz it! Come on, giz a loosie!

OLD SHEFFIELD CHANT IN THREE PARTS

1. Nar den D
   R da guin on?
2. RD R8? R?
3. Shut di gob or a'll chin D!

(to be done as a round in a pub late at night until the coppers come)

lop *noun* a flea

loppy *adjective* flea-ridden

> By gum I'm feeling loppy

> *This last to be muttered while*
> *scratching one's belly with the neb of*
> *one's cap*

lops *plural noun* guts

lowence *noun* a snack taken to work, esp by a
farmer [from *allowence*]

> Don't forget thi lowence Clarence!

lownd *noun* *spoken in West Yorkshire* a gentle
Spring rain

> I was strolling in the lownd
> along the Yorkshire ground (Coleridge)*

> *This is one of the most beautiful words*
> *in Yorkshire Dialect, especially when*

> *you hear it pattering on your umbrella*
> *during a stroll in the Dales*

mafted *adjective* (of a person) suffering under the heat

> Turn that electric fire down: I'm mafted!

> *Somehow seems to suggest the rubbing*
> *of tight underwear against skin in hot*
> *weather*

manky *adjective* unpleasant in smell, taste, or appearance

> them chips were manky all right

> *Also used as a noun, like 'That room is*
> *full of mank' so that the smell takes on*
> *a solid physical appearance and*
> *possibly a green hue and a low hum.*

mardy *adjective* moody or irritable [from marred,

past participle of mar, which means to spoil].
Also **maungey**

> Oh that mardy git. He's allus got the monk on abaht summat!

> *I try not to be mardy, but you should see me when Barnsley have lost or I've just missed a bus or somebody has driven past a puddle in a 4X4 and splashed my kecks.*

mash *verb* (of tea) to brew

> Do you want your tea yet?
> No, love, let it mash a while.

> *I guess that mash can only really be used with leaf tea rather than teabags.*

maungey *adjective* Same as **mardy**

Oh that maungey git. He's allus got the monk on abaht summat!

I think that maungey is mardier than mardy.

mend *verb* to add fuel to (a fire or stove)

Mend that fire will tha'? Why, are tha nesh?

I love the idea of a broken fire that has to be mended with coal before it can give us heat.

Mester *noun* Mister

If you don't stop chucking radishes I'll tell that mester!

misteched *adjective* (of a person) having fallen into bad habits

That vicar's misteched since he joined that graffiti crew!

Another example of that mixture of onomatopoeia and Yorkshireness which at least one commentator calls Yorkomatopoeia

mither *verb* to bother; pester

> Stop mithering your dad when he's trying to read his Derrida!

moider *verb* *South Yorkshire version of* **mither**

> Tha better stop moidering me, lad

monk *noun* **have the monk on** to sulk

> If tha's got the monk on again I'm stoppin' in

mowdiwarp *or* **moldiwarp** *noun* a mole (the burrowing animal)

> 'The clouds are coming over like mowdiwarp skins' (Ted Hughes – not really)
>
> *Mowdiwarp Challenge: an old West*

*Yorkshire game to see how many
anagrams one can make from the word
in the time it takes a mole to dig a new
molehill.*

mun *verb* must; used to express obligation

Tha mun do it thissen!

*There aren't that many South Yorkshire
words with the letter S at the end; I
reckon some South Yorkshire folks
consider it fey and southern to
pronounce your Ss.*

nap *spoken in North Yorkshire noun* the lighter
colour of tilled soil as it dries out | *verb* (of soil)
to take on this appearance

Aye, it's starting to nap ower nicely

neb *noun* the front of a flat cap

Neb on his cap like the continental shelf!

The equivalent of a Swiss Army knife for a Yorkshireman. Can be used for cooling tea by wafting, getting into a locked house, scratching the neck, and swatting flies. Neb can also mean nose, so we are really talking about the front of the flat cap looking a bit like a nose. Although I wouldn't want to meet anybody who had a nose like the front of a flat cap.

nesh *adjective* overly sensitive to the cold [from old English hnesce]

What's tha doin wi' that muffler? Are that nesh?

Because I've used this word all my life

in certain wintry situations, I start to
shiver as soon as I see it written down
or hear it said. Pavlov's Tyke!

nithered *adjective* feeling very cold

By, I'm nithered watching this not very
interesting game of amateur Rugby League!

nobbut *adverb* just; only [a minimalising of
nothing but. Never use two words when one will
do. Or neverusetwowordswhenonewilldo]

he's nobbut a doll's eead, that bloke!

From 'nothing but'. Another
Yorkshire cliché word that remains
alive and well and impervious to
metropolitan sneering. (You know
who you are.)

nowt *noun* nothing

I had nowt to do wi' that, son, that was all your mam

Yorkshire Confucius say: 'Hear all, see all, say nowt; and if tha does owt for nowt, do it for thissen!'

now then *interjection* hello

Now then fatha! Are tha guin to't ale oil?

A very odd locution, if examined under a strong light. 'How do?' makes more sense.

ower *preposition* over

gie ower wi' that racket – tha's mithering Uncle Bob.

owt *noun* anything

Doin 'owt this evening?

The opposite of nowt

SCENE FROM 'BRIEF ENCOUNTER' IN THE ORIGINAL YORKSHIRE

He: Nar then!

She: Shurrup!

He: What's up wi thi?

She: Shurrup!

He: What tha rooarin for? Are tha nesh?

She: Av got summat in me een!

He: Duz tha want a barm cake in't caff?

She: Can tha get this thing art o'me een?
     Feels like I've gorra grod in theer!

pafalled *adjective spoken in North Yorkshire* very tired; exhausted

> Carrying that harpsichord up to Granma's room has left me fair pafalled!

> *One of those words that would almost take too long to say if you were the thing the word was describing, if you get my drift.*

paggered *adjective* very tired; knackered

> Carrying that spinet up to Grandad's room has left me fair paggered!

> *Although, it must be said, paggers are not knackers...*

piggin *noun spoken in Huddersfield* metal container

> Don't put pigeon in't piggin piggin! Basket's ower here.

pike *noun* a look or glance

Have a pike at that!

*Another word still in common use;
somehow I reckon it must be a
corruption of peep.*

pikelet *noun* a crumpet

*Reached its zenith at my auntie's house
one Sunday afternoon in 1966 on a fork
in front of the fire just before Sing
Something Simple came on. It was a
clear Autumn night, and Winter was
waiting in the wings.*

pisspotical *adjective spoken in South Yorkshire*
ridiculous

That's a pisspotical way to rewire an old folks'
bungalow.

I heard this a lot on the building site I used to work at in Sheffield in the 1970s. I guess it means 'something so ridiculous you wouldn't piss it into a pot'. Arthur on the building site used to say bodokulous *rather than 'ridiculous', but that was that branch-line of Yorkshire dialect known as 'words only spoken by one bloke in a cap'.*

pobby *adjective spoken in South Yorkshire* (of a person) soft or weak

That boyfriend o' thine's a bit pobby, in't he? He could onny manage sixteen pints at' t'club!'

pop *noun* **play pop** to reprimand severely; tell off

Dad'll play pop with me when he finds out I've lost his S Club Seven boxed set

Very polite, this one. Pop here is a polite

word for 'hell', which is usually a polite
word for something else...

powfagged *adjective* (of a person) fatigued;
exhausted

> I'm proper powfagged after doin't London
> Marathon dressed as Dickie Bird!

> *Although you'd have to have quite a bit*
> *of energy to say it.*

powl *verb* **be powled** *spoken in Linthwaite* have
one's hair cut

> Has ter bin powled?

puther *noun* smoke, especially thick smoke
issuing from a fire that you've just lit. It could be
that there's a pigeon stuck up the chimney.

> There's a right puther in here: have you been
> smoking loosies?

TRADITIONAL YORKSHIRE SKIPPING RHYME THAT I JUST MADE UP

Claart-heead, doll's head
Wear thi daddy's brat!

Coil oil, chip oil
Have a skeg at that!

TRANSLATION, WHICH DOESN'T WORK QUITE SO WELL

You fool, you fool,
Put your father's apron on.

Coal bunker, fish and chip shop,
Look at that.

quack *noun spoken in West Ardsley, West Yorkshire*
  a segment of orange

> Pass us a sliver of quack, old fruit.

> *A lovely word with a very specific*
> *geographical setting; localness is*
> *alive and well and living in*
> *Yorkshire language!*

radged *adjective* very angry; raging

> He were radged when he fon art that somebody
> had pinched the booit out of his Rotherham
> Monopoly!

rammel *noun* rubbish; debris

> *A teenager's bedroom can also be*
> *known as a 'rammel station'*

recklin *noun* the weakest of the litter; runt

> That Ringo were't recklin of' t' Beatles

reek *noun* smoke

> There's a reyt reek in yon rooim!

reyt *adjective, adverb* really

> Tha're a doll's eead reyt!

An extremely useful, bicycle spanner of a word.

rheeubub *noun* rhubarb

> he had hair like a field of rheeubub!

Often heard in the stygian darkness of the forcing sheds in the rhubarb triangle.

riding *noun* any of the three former administrative divisions of Yorkshire

> He's West Riding through and through: you can tell by the way the neb of his cap shines in't dark...

From the old English word thriding,
from the Old Norse for 'third'. It used to
be North Thriding, East Thriding, and
West Thriding until years of use in
Yorkshire, where no-one says more
than he has to, finally wore away the
initial 'th'.

rop *noun* a paunch; beer belly

Did that rop come with that shirt?

I was once walking down a street in
Doncaster when someone shouted this
at me from the top deck of a bus

saar oil *noun* *spoken in Wakefield* a grating
outside the back door of a house

I've dropped my house keys darn't saar oil on my
way om from't chip oil...

Most likely from 'sewer hole'

TYKE HAIKU

Neet: nutty slack black;
Black as coil oil or crozzley
Till't pudding mooin.

(Night is as black as certain kinds of coal; indeed it's as black as the place we keep the coal, or the overdone crackling from a pork joint.)

(However, once the moon comes out, light and round like a Yorkshire Pudding , the sky lightens.)

sackless *adjective* not very clever

> You sackless nowt!

> *Also means 'innocent'. Gorm can be*
> *used as a noun, but sack can't. You can*
> *say 'She took no gorm of him' but you*
> *can't say 'she took no sack of him'*

sam *noun* **give someone a sam up** *spoken in*
North Yorkshire to help (someone) to climb or
look over an obstacle, esp by joining locking
one's hands together to form a step

> Gis a sam up ower this wall, will thi, our gert's
> comin'!

scallion *noun* shallot

> Does tha want a scallion wi that ice cream or are
> tha just pretendin to be eccentric?

> *Rapscallion: hip hop rhythm created by*
> *banging two shallots together.*

scran *noun* food

> I'm gaggin for a bit o'scran!

seeat *noun* seat

> When I go am gunner have a seeat put up for me in't park!

Another pronunciation that Yorkshire folk seem to want to alter just for the heck of it.

seeat *noun* soot

seg *noun* a metal stud inserted in the sole of a shoe to keep it from wearing away

> My chips always taste like segs!

Of course these days we can see nose segs, nipple segs and unmentionable segs.

sen *noun* the self; the inner being

I felt badly on me sen

A branch of contemplation in Yorkshire could be called Sen Buddhism, looking deep into your inner sen.

serry *interjection* my good sir!

Nar then, serry, what can ah do for thi?

this is a corruption of the old-fashioned and spectacularly posh 'Sirrah!' My father in law used it and it is often confused with sithee which is in fact nothing like it.

shack *verb* to shake

Come, on shack thissen art of bed; t'Bishop's coming!

A fine example of Yorkshire Shortening,

making a tiny word tinier.

shacked *adjective* shaken

I were reyt shacked when Bishop turned up!

sithi *interjection* look here

Look at this bruise on mi leg, sithi!

Not to be used to mean 'I'll see you later'; this usage was coined by the late Fred Truman on his ITV teatime show Indoor League *when, at the end of the programme, he would remove the pipe from his mouth, take a sip of his beer, and say 'I'll sithi!' Not to be confused with serry (see above), although you could have the phrase 'sithi serry' which could mean 'Look here my good man!'*

HESITANT YORKSHIRE DECLARATION OF LOVE

Tha sees, tha knows, semmas,
Reyt, I love thi mooar than mi mam's
Parkin. A lot mooar. Her parkin's loppy.

(You see, you know, same as I've just told you, right, I love you more than I love my mam's ginger cake. A lot more. Her ginger cake tastes like it's infested with fleas.)

skeg *noun* a look or glance

> have a skeg at that

skelbeease *noun* a division in a cowshed

> Make sure than unruly cow doesn't get in the wrong skelbeease.

I like words that are almost impossible to use to mean anything else.

sken *verb* squint or stare

> I'll just have a sken at the paper before I do my ironing

skerrick *noun* *spoken in South Yorkshire* a small amount [A word that sounds like what it means. One imagines that something smaller than a *skerrick* would be a *skerrickette*, and something larger than a *skerrick* would be a *sker*]

> Just drizzle a skerrick of alicker on that tripe

I always thought my wife had made this up. My mate Keith reckons it should be skerrit, but what does he know? He's not my wife!

skrike *verb* to cry

She were skrikin like a babby!

I reckon this could come from squawk, don't you?

skyme *verb* to give a furtive glance at

I reckon you skyme best with your collar up.

slaipe *adjective spoken in Harrogate* slippery

Mind thissen; yon path's reyt slaipe, unless you're in Skipton or Keighley; anywhere but Harrogate in fact.

slantendicular *adjective* just off the perpendicular

Uncle Frank ended up slantendicular on his birthday.

Another example of a word in very narrow use.

slart *spoken in South Yorkshire* *verb* to rain

It's guin' t'slart

It seems to me this word has the additional quality of describing the shape of raindrops making their way down a mucky pane. As in the Yorkshire poem: We're all darn in't coil oil Wheer muck slarts on't winders Bum baliff'll nivver finnd us...

slutch *noun* mud

Don't walk on my new carpet; you're all clarted up wi slutch.

Slutch is less sloppy than slap dab or

slop dosh.

smit *verb* to mark sheep

> Has tha seen mi smitting brush?

smitten *adjective* pregnant

> She's been smitten by't millkman's lad!

There's a variation of this: smickled. I prefer that, but only because it comes from my locality.

sneg *verb* to fish from a pier using a simple line

> I've just been sneggin: I got a couple of dogfish!

snek *noun* a door latch

> Don't forget to put't snek down when you go to't club!

snicket *noun* a passageway between houses. *Also* **ginnel**, **jennel**, **tenfoot** and **spritehouse**. I made that last one up.

TYKERICK WITH TRANSLATION

A gormless young feller from Ull
Said 'My marrer is sackless and dull
He can't fettle nowt reyt
And he's slack in a feyt
He's a doll's 'ead, a rattlin' skull!'

(A not very bright teenaged boy from the East Coast
remarked that his friend was equally unintelligent and
lacked any kind of spark or charisma; he was no good at
mending things and was certainly no practical helpin a
bout of fisticuffs. In fact there was some speculation as to
whether he had a brain at all.)

Spanish *noun* liquorice

> Giz a chow o' thi Spanish.

> *We had a teacher at school called Mr Liquorice. Of course we asked him if he taught allsorts! Of course we asked him if he taught Spanish! You would expect nothing else of schoolboys!*

spelk *noun* a splinter [from old English *spelt* surgical splint]

> I've gorra spelk in my thumb like a yule log.

> *You can also call it a spell, without the T, if it's a smaller spelk or a spelkette.*

spice *noun* sweets

> Giz one of thi spice!

> *Another word that I didn't realise was dialect. Am I naive or what?*

spuggy *noun* a sparrow

> Flocks of spuggies whirling round in't sky like tealeaves in a cup!

staddle *noun* a frame for a haystack

> My haystack's floppy because I forgot my staddle.

starved *adjective* (of a person) very cold

> Riddle: When can a fat bloke be starved? Answer: When he's from Yorkshire

steggle *verb spoken in North Yorkshire* to walk about craning the neck as if looking for something

> What tha stegglin' like a giraffe for?

stoop *noun* a milestone, gatepost, etc

> Turn left at that stoop, and then tha'll be theer!

I once walked past an old chap of my acquaintance on the street and didn't

say Good Morning to him. He shouted:
'Tha walked past me like I were a
stoop!'

summat *pronoun, adverb* something

Tha nesh or summat?

Me back hurts summat awful

sup *verb* **1** to drink | *noun* **2** a drink

We've supped some stuff tonight.

I always think that this is a word that
builds in the possibility of spillage
down a cardigan.

swarf *noun* mixture of grease and grit

I can't get this swarf off my hands when I've
done a double shift!

It must be a real word because you can
buy Swarfega™ to get it off.

tapper *noun* an unstable and violent man

> Watch out for that tapper on the top deck.

tarn *noun* lake or pond

> Are you going swimming in't tarn?

> *I got told off in the letters page of my local paper for suggesting that tarn was Barnsley for town. I stand corrected!*

tatahash *noun* cheap stew

> Tatahash for dinner toneet! Lovely!

> *Unless you're posh, in which case you have potato casserole.*

teem *verb* to pour (tea)

> Teem that tea for't team, Doreen.

thissen *pronoun* yourself

I'm not gerrin it: gerrit thissen.

Gerrit Thissen does sound like a
Scandinavian Sound Artist to me.

thraip *vb* to be thrashed; thoroughly defeated
 > **thraiping** *n*

We got thraiped 12–0

There's a great bit in Billy Liar where
Billy and his mate are talking to daft
bluff old Yorkshire councillor and they
talk in Yorkshire nonsense, of which the
word thraiped is a major part...

throit *noun* throat

Is thi clack too big for thi throit?

Well, if coat is coit then it follows that
throat should be throit. But why is goat
never goit?

YORKSHIRE AS SURREALIST CAPITAL OF THE WORLD

The biggerstang on the town hall
Smells of cleg
Or fent.

A scutch
Makes it fleg
To the floor.

Biggerstang collapse
Makes dust like kahli

Bits fall off the town hall
Like cog
Like quack.

throng *adjective* busy

> eee, it were throng in't fishmarket when't squid lorry came in.

tipple *verb* to cause (something) to fall over

> Our Frank tippled oer on Nanny Marr road.

> *Feel the word itself tipple as you write it, read it, and say it!*

tow *verb* **tow one's lops out** to work extremely hard. *See* **lops**

> Whaddya mean laikin'? Ah been towin' me lops out!

tranklements *plural noun* One's favourite (small) possessions

trowthit *noun* stile between two fields of unequal heights

> I tore mu kex on Farmer Lancashire's trowthit.

I love the ancient feel of this word: like
loam between my stubby fingers.

trump *verb* to fart

Who trumped in the quiet part of the Trout
Quintet?

A word that is intrinsically funny, no
matter who or where or what you are.

twa *determiner* two

unch *adjective* *spoken in coastal areas of Yorkshire*
cold

Unch today – I'm froz

From being hunched over on the front
at Whitby, trying to keep out the cold.

watter *noun, verb* water

There's watter com through't ceiling!

wesh *verb* wash

> I didn't bother wi a bath but I had a good wesh at't sink.

while *adverb* until

winter hedge *noun* a clothes horse

> Pants and vests in a line on the Winter Hedge, lined up like seagulls and the sails of pirate ships.

wuthering *adjective* blowing strongly with a roaring wind

yam *noun* *spoken in North Yorkshire*

> I'm gan yam wi mi mam and our sam for some ham and jam.

> *In South Yorkshire we say 'ooam'. So you can imagine a Beckettian dialogue between two people from opposite ends of Yorkshire. He: Am gan yam. She: Am*

gooin ooam He: A thowt yer wa gannin yam! She: Reyt. Am gooin ooam! The introduction of a person from North Derbyshire would then show the innate dignity of the Yorkshire Dialect. Derbyshire: Am gooin to my arse! He: A thowt yer wa gannin yam! She: Ah thowt that woh gooin ooam! Derbyshire: Ah've had a brick extension put on my arse!

yesst *noun* yeast. *Also* **barm**

yitten *adjective* frightened

I'm yitten to go in that haunted arse in Chesterfield!